The World's Greatest

Volume 55

by

Ted Gambordella

Allen Steen

CHAMPIONS
1960 - 1970's

World's Greatest Martial Artists

Allen Steen　　Jamie Cashion　　Gary Lee　　Mark Shuey　　Michael DePasquale

Linda Denley　　Bill Wallace　　Ismael Robles　　Ted Gambordella　　Keith Vitali

Pat Burleson　　Troy Dorsey　　Joe Corley　　Rudy Smedley　　Andrew Linick

Keith Yates　　Jeff Smith　　George Minshew　　Ray McCallum　　Jim Thomas

Advisory Board

The World's Greatest Martial Artists

1. Adam Martin
2. Adam Octavian
3. Adrian Valman
4. Alcides Villacampa
5. Alick Smith
6. Allen Hurd
7. Alonso Rosado
8. Anthony Miles
9. Berthony Pascal
10. Bill Gray
11. Bill Logan
12. Brad Marshall
13. Brian Ayotte
14. Bryan Griffin
15. Carroll Baker
16. Charles Goodman
17. Chuck Vaughn
18. Cy Stearns
19. Dave Gentry
20. David Chaanine
21. David L. Wynn
22. David Lewis
23. Daz Stirrat
24. Deb Harris-Krezel
25. Del Rounds
26. Don Padge Padgett
27. Efrain Valentin
28. Fariborz Azhakh
29. Filipe da Conceição.
30. Flores Vincent
31. Francisco Sánchez García
32. Frank Noel Viñas Campos
33. Geoff MacDonald
34. Han Wong
35. Hans Demant
36. Harold E. Gibbs Jr.
37. Jae-yoon An
38. Jeff Gibbs
39. Jeremy S. Hughes
40. Jinho Guahk
41. John McGonigle Sr.
42. Jorge Eduardo Araiza
43. Jose Luis Montes
44. Joseph L. Sessum
45. Josh Moree
46. Kalla Bergers
47. Ken Marchtaler
48. Kenneth Hill Jr.
49. Kevin Grissom
50. Kevin Schoenebeck
51. Kyle Forrest
52. Lady-Lallaine Reed
53. Leslie Kaiser
54. Lionel Edwards
55. Lonnie Lockridge
56. Lorne Bernard
57. Mario Alem
58. Mario Bellerino
59. Mark D Bishop
60. Mark Johnson
61. Marques McCammon
62. Márton László
63. Matthew Thammavong
64. Mike Green
65. Moises Rivera Barreto
66. Mwanzo Mwalimu Umeme
67. Norman Bivens
68. Paul Robert Pears
69. Pedro Adão
70. Peter Paik
71. Peter Sorce
72. Rafael Ubri
73. Ramcana Hastings
74. Ramón S Aliaga
75. Rick Manglinong
76. Rob Davidson
77. Robert Haas
78. Robert Jackson
79. Robert Taylor
80. Roberto Serrano
81. Roger Boggs
82. Rony Kluger
83. Roy Faiga
84. Sabrina Heidemann
85. Scott Packard
86. Serge Armand Fegain Fewo
87. Shlomo David
88. Silverio P. Guerra
89. Sonny Pillay
90. Steve Fitzgerald.
91. Tadashi Yamashita
92. Tedd O'Neill
93. Thomas Hardie
94. Tom Vo
95. Tony D'Angelo
96. Tony Diaz
97. Tony Pelay
98. Vic Theriault
99. Vince Cassar
100. Virgil Allen
101. Young Lee

The World's Greatest Martial Artists

Adam Martin

Adam Octavian

The World's Greatest Martial Artists

Adrian Valman

MARTIAL ARTS MASTERS
HALL OF FAME

PaiLum.org

White Dragon Warrior Society
International Conference 2021
www.pailum.org

Alcides Villacampa

The World's Greatest Martial Artists

Alick Smith

Roger Hurd

Allen Hurd

The World's Greatest Martial Artists

Alonso Rosado

The World's Greatest Martial Artists

Anthony Miles

The World's Greatest Martial Artists

Berthony Pascal

Bill Gray

The World's Greatest Martial Artists

Bill Logan

The World's Greatest Martial Artists

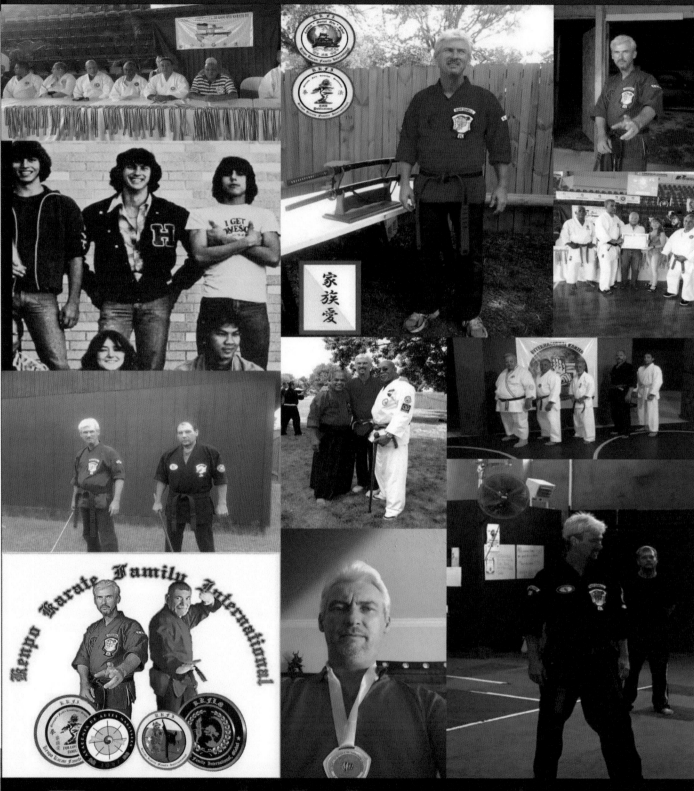

Brad Marshall

The World's Greatest Martial Artists

Brian Ayotte

The World's Greatest Martial Artists

Bryan Griffin

The World's Greatest Martial Artists

Carroll Baker

MARTIAL ARTS MASTERS
HALL OF FAME

Charles Goodman

16

The World's Greatest Martial Artists

Chuck Vaughn

Cy Stearns

MARTIAL ARTS MASTERS HALL OF FAME

Dave Gentry

The World's Greatest Martial Artists

David Chaanine

The World's Greatest Martial Artists

HALL OF HONOR

GM DAVID WYNN
You have been nominated to be honored at
the 2022 Who's Who In Martial Arts International
Honor Night Of Honors / Saturday April 23rd 2022
at the Royal Hall 613 Hope Rd Eatontown New Jersey
event will start at 6:pm sharp

David L. Wynn

21

David Lewis

The World's Greatest Martial Artists

Daz Stirrat

MARTIAL ARTS MASTERS HALL OF FAME

Deb Harris-Krezel

The World's Greatest Martial Artists

Edinboro Family Martial Arts Center

The U.S.A. KARATE FEDERATION CORPORATE OFFICES National Governing Body For Amateur KARATE OF THE UNITED STATES OF AMERICA

Del Rounds

Don Padge Padgett

The World's Greatest Martial Artists

Efrain Valentin

The World's Greatest Martial Artists

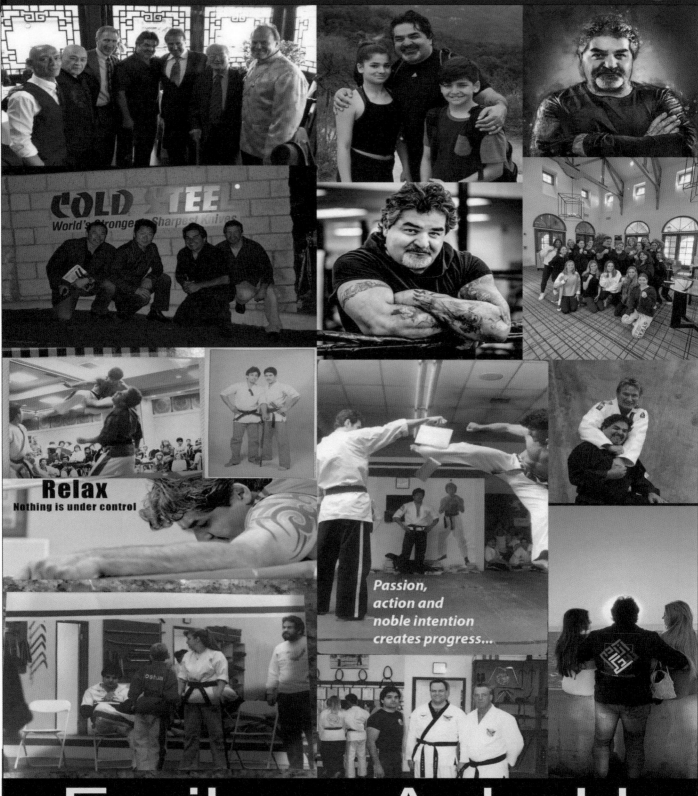

Relax
Nothing is under control

Passion,
action and
noble intention
creates progress...

Fariborz Azhakh

Filipe da Conceição

Flores Vincent

Francisco Sánchez García

The World's Greatest Martial Artists

Frank Noel Viñas Campos

The World's Greatest Martial Artists

Geoff MacDonald

The World's Greatest Martial Artists

YOU'RE NEVER TOO OLD OR TOO YOUNG TO LEARN!

Three ages of Sport

⊙ 2 YEARS AGO

ONCE UPON A TIME
I STAND ON THE WINNING PODIUM
TO COLLECT MY TROPHY FROM...

GM HAN WONG (GB)

LIFETIME
ACHIEVEMENT

Salon 龍沙

Han Wong

34

MARTIAL ARTS MASTERS
HALL OF FAME

JUKU RYU JU JITSU
SELVFORSVARS KLUBBER

UNITED NATIONS
OF JU JITSU

DANSK JU-JITSU FORBUND

Hans Demant

The World's Greatest Martial Artists

Harold E. Gibbs Jr.

The World's Greatest Martial Artists

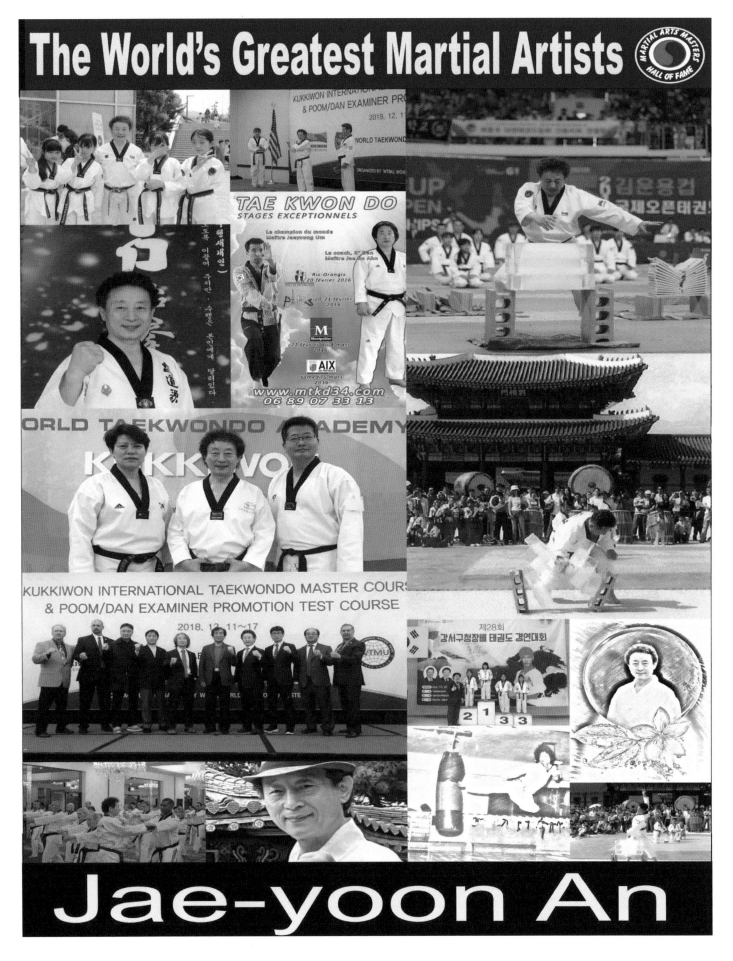

Jae-yoon An

Jeff Gibbs

The World's Greatest Martial Artists

To my Brother in the Arts

WELCOM

Jeremy S. Hughes

The World's Greatest Martial Artists

APPRECIATION PLAQUE

MR. JIN HO GUAHK
Grand Master
Hapkido Moohak-Kwan

IN APPRECIATION FOR YOUR DEDICATED SERVICE
AS A PRESENTER IN 2019 AUSTRALIAN HAPKIDO
INSTRUCTOR SEMINAR IN
SYDNEY AUSTRALIA

13 October 2019

SUNG SOO LEE
PRESIDENT
AUSTRALIA HAPKIDO FEDERATION

Jinho Guahk

The World's Greatest Martial Artists

John McGonigle Sr.

Jorge Eduardo Araiza

The World's Greatest Martial Artists

JOSÉ LUIS MONTES
PRESIDENT OF WISDA, UWAMA AND ITIPA

GRANDMASTER 8 DAN IN POLICE SELF DEFENCE
GRANDMASTER 8 DAN IN TAIHO JUTSU
MASTER IN KICK BOXING, MUAY THAI,
JIU JITSU, KARATE, SAMBO...
3 TIMES WORLD CHAMPION IN SELF DEFENCE
EUROPEAN POLICE CHAMPION IN KARATE
EUROPEAN CHAMPION IN POLICE BATON COMBAT
PRESIDENT BARCELONA HALL OF HONORS SAMURAI AWARDS
PRESIDENT THE 100 BEST MARTIAL ARTIST IN THE WORLD

Aprende a defenderte con el campeón del mundo de defensa personal Jose Luis Montes

Jose Luis Montes

43

The World's Greatest Martial Artists

May this season find you among those you love, sharing in the twin glories of generosity and gratitude.

Love,
Joseph

Joseph L. Sessum

The World's Greatest Martial Artists

Josh Moree

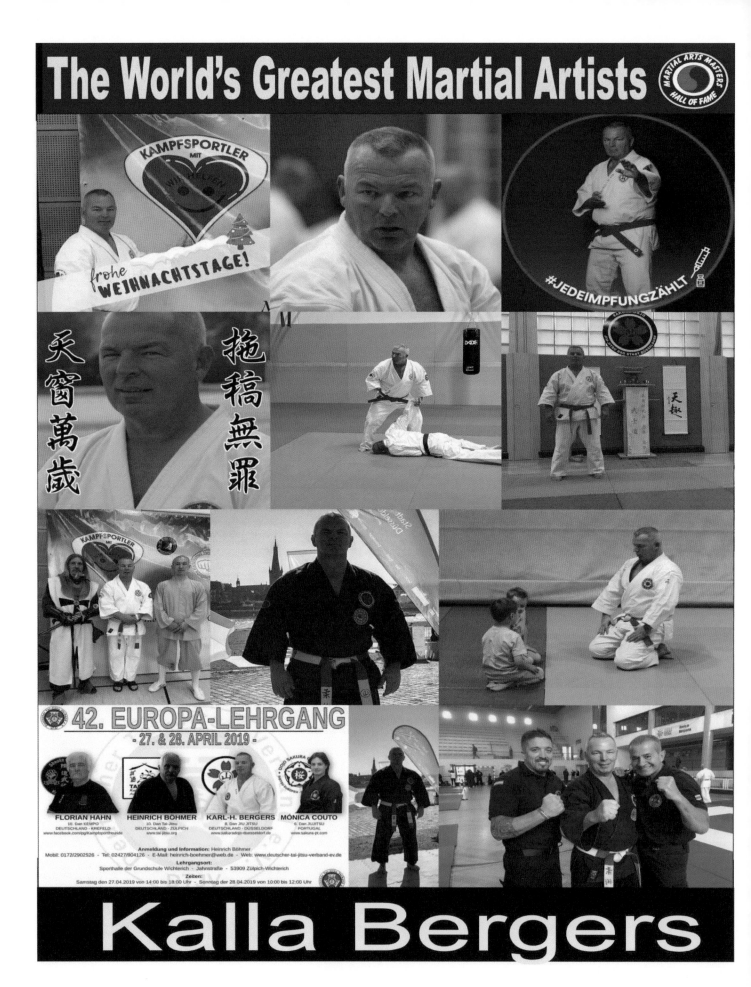

The World's Greatest Martial Artists

Ken Marchtaler

Kenneth Hill Jr.

Photo of instructing Mr. Kevin Grissom with Push-hand and Ta-lu who is coach of King Kung-fu Studio, inc. in Waukegan, Illinois.

Kevin Grissom

The World's Greatest Martial Artists

MARTIAL ARTS MASTERS HALL OF FAME

Martial Arts to fit YOU

TOTAL SELF DEFENSE
920-737-5417
www.TSDSuccess.com

Kevin Schoenebeck

Kyle Forrest

The World's Greatest Martial Artists

Lady-Lallaine Reed

Leslie Kaiser

Lionel Edwards

Lonnie Lockridge

Lorne Bernard

The World's Greatest Martial Artists

Mario Alem

Mario Bellerino

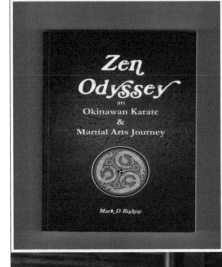

KARATE, KOBUDO & TE

Self-Defence Applications Decoded

Mark D Bishop

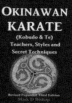

Mark D Bishop

The World's Greatest Martial Artists

Grandmaster Mark Johnson, 8th Dan, LMT, CMT, B/

Battle of Atlanta Black Belt Hall of Fame, 2007
Who's Who Legends Award, 2015
AFKA Hall of Fame, Chiefmaster Instructor Award, 20
US Head of Family Martial Arts Assoc., Master of Hon
US Head of Family Martial Arts Assoc., Lifetime Mem
US Head of Family Martial Arts Assoc., CA State Rep.

STRICTLY

BUSIN

Mark Johnson

The World's Greatest Martial Artists

March/31/998

Marques McCammon

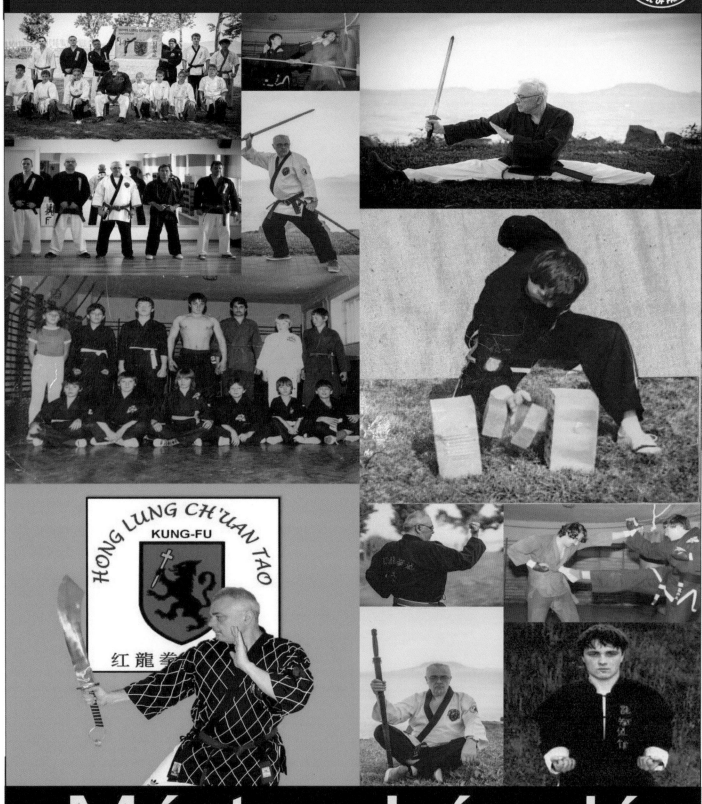

HONG LUNG CH'UAN TAO
KUNG-FU
红龍拳

Márton László

The World's Greatest Martial Artists

Matthew Thammavong

Mike Green

The World's Greatest Martial Artists

Hall of Famer GM MoisesRivera

2022 2023

Moises Rivera Barreto

The World's Greatest Martial Artists

Mwanzo Mwalimu Umeme

The World's Greatest Martial Artists

Norman Bivens

MARTIAL ARTS MASTERS HALL OF FAME

MASTER PAUL PEARS

MASTER PAUL PEARS

COALITION OF ANCESTRAL MARTIAL ARTS INTERNATIONAL
UNITED KINGDOM

WTKA G
ENGLAND SCOTLAND
IRELAND WALES

MASTER PAUL PEARS & MASTER IAN PARKER

Paul Robert Pears

The World's Greatest Martial Artists

WEDNESDAY · TOGETHER WE CAN

SAKURA TEAM

Pedro Adão

The World's Greatest Martial Artists

Peter Paik

MARTIAL ARTS MASTERS
HALL OF FAME

Peter Sorce

Rafael Ubri

Hanshi Ramoana Hastings

Ramón S Aliaga

The World's Greatest Martial Artists

Confirmed Camp Instructors

Parsons - Michigan

LaCava - Connecticut

Manglinong - California

Vigoroux - NY & Chile

Espinous - France

Giron - California

Rick Manglinong

Rob Davidson

The World's Greatest Martial Artists

Robert Haas

Robert Jackson

Robert Taylor

The World's Greatest Martial Artists

BILL SALANO - JOHN TOWNSLEY
ROB SERRANO - DEAN LASSITER

New Year, Better You! Time to get into Class!

MAA

DEAN LASSITER   ROBERTO SERRANO, Jr.   RICHARD RYAN   ARLENE LIMAS   JOE LEWIS   ROGER GREENE   DAVID SIXEL

JOHN TOWNSLEY   WALT LYSAK, Jr.

TEAM USA MASTER CLASS SEMINAR

Roberto Serrano

MARTIAL ARTS MASTERS HALL OF FAME

Roger Boggs

The World's Greatest Martial Artists

Rony Kluger

The World's Greatest Martial Artists

Ultimate Karate
International Martial Arts Seminar
May 16, 2015

Roy Faiga

The World's Greatest Martial Artists

Sabrina Heidemann

The World's Greatest Martial Artists

PACKARD'S MARTIAL ARTS

Scott Packard

Serge Armand Fegain Fewo

Shlomo David

The World's Greatest Martial Artists

Molina presents Professor Silverio P. Guerra with his induction into the prestigious Mexican MMA Hall of Fame.

UMAHoF 28TH ANNUAL EVENT

The UMAHOF 28th annual event will be held at the Houston South Marriott by Houston Hobby Airport on the 10th - 12th Aug 2023. For more information call Professor Guerra at (832)701-3427.

10TH AUG - 12TH AUG, 2023

UMAHOF 28TH ANNUAL EVENT
HOUSTON SOUTH MARRIOTT BY HOUSTON HOBBY AIRPORT

REGISTER TODAY

More Information (832)701-3427

Silverio P. Guerra

MARTIAL ARTS MASTERS
HALL OF FAME

SKIF ...HAPING TH...
ESTB. 1978
SHOTOKAN KARATE-DO-INTERNATIONAL SOUTH AFRICA
...ATE-D... ...RNATIONAL ...UTH AFRICA
SHOTOKAN KARA...
...SO...

HOME ...THE CHAMP...

AFFILIATE... ...SKIF (JAPAN)   KS...

Karate siblings flying high

OWN CORRESPONDENT

SISTERS Zia Omera Pillay (15) and Azaria Imani Pillay (14) of Malvern will represent SA at the World Championships in Konya, Turkey from October 26-30.

The duo, who have been doing karate for the past nine years, are first dan (shodan) black belt holders and have achieved their world rankings in karate.

They are both capped Proteas and have represented the country in international events.

The World Championships are second only to the Olympics, and only the number one pick from each country is allowed participation.

Renshi Brando Pillay, the technical convenor of Karate SA, has personally trained and mentored these karatekas to prepare them to compete at this level.

FROM left, Zia Pillay, Renshi Brando Pillay, and Azaria Pillay. | Supplied

I GOT MY COVID-19 VACCINE
UNICEF

Sonny Pillay

Steve Fitzgerald

The World's Greatest Martial Artists

EFFECTIVE IMPROVISATION. A new ruling by the state of California that has banned the nunchaku in California didn't prevent Tadashi Yamashita (above) from performing one of his favorite demonstrations. He used a belt instead.

小林流

KARATE & KIDS

Hollywood heavyweight demonstrates his chops

KUNG-FU

Angular Attack

Tadashi Yamashita

Tedd O'Neill

Thomas Hardie

The World's Greatest Martial Artists

Tom Vo

Tony D'Angelo

Tony Diaz Shihan

Will Be Attending!

Tony Diaz

The World's Greatest Martial Artists

Tony Pelay

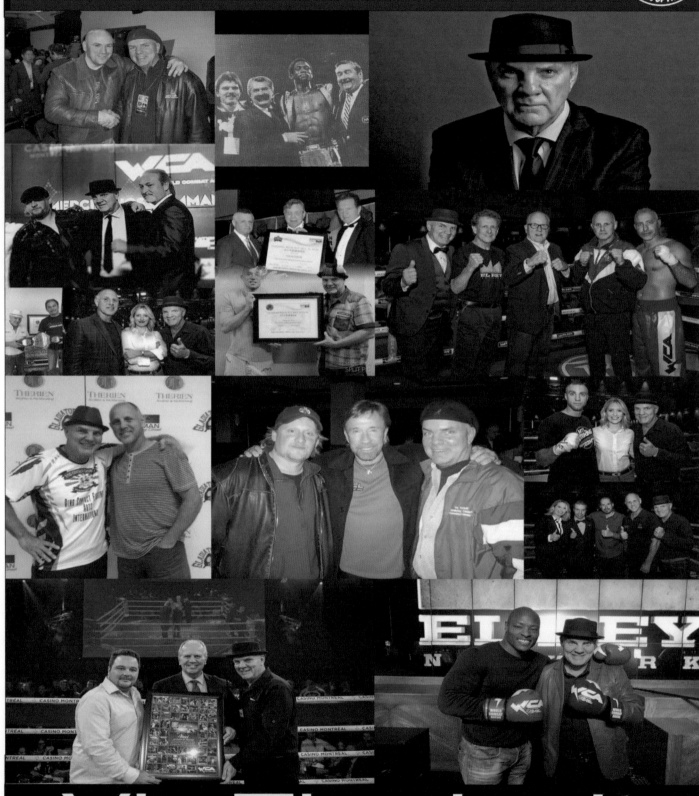

Vic Theriault

The World's Greatest Martial Artists

Vince Cassar

The World's Greatest Martial Artists

Virgil Allen

MARTIAL ARTS MASTERS HALL OF FAME

Young Lee